Belly Shame: Stories from the Gut

Edited by Debra DeAngelo and David Lacy

iPinion Syndicate Publications
iPinion Syndicate, LLC

Thank you for purchasing "Belly Shame: Stories from the Gut," iPinion Syndicate's first publication. Your purchase will help pay our bills and fund our website, which is a collective of accomplished and award-winning writers, photographers and artists, sharing their disparate thoughts, beliefs, humor, imagery, world-views, rants, diatribes, useless banter, substantive insights, ideological B.S., and perhaps sometimes odd outlooks on life. No columnist's view necessarily reflects that of any other columnist nor the views of iPinion Syndicate, LLC.

CONTENTS

Do you have the guts?

DAVID LACY

iPinion Syndicate contributors were challenged to share their thoughts and experiences on body shame and, in particular, that one part of our bodies that no one seems to be happy with: our bellies. Whether fit or fat, thin or thick, many of us look at our midsections and feel self-loathing and despair.

While we were aware that many of our writers had struggled with body image issues (as some of them had written publicly about these on prior occasions), my iPinion co-founder Debra DeAngelo and I were frankly taken aback by the levels of obsessive thinking — frequently bordering on compulsive — that many in the group had given to their stomachs. Women and men, young and old, shared powerful stories that were at once tremendously unique to each individual and simultaneously made common by that most insidious emotion: shame.

I myself have been chubby, average weight, and yardstick-thin during different periods in my 35 year-life The latter was a result of a six-year battle with male anorexia, followed by a leap into exercise bulimia. And I'll be blunt: Before I read my colleagues' work, I didn't think they'd be able to offer me much that I didn't already know and feel personally about the pain of staring in a mirror and hating my reflection. Even a day before I set about editing this anthology, I didn't recognize just how ubiquitous many of these experiences were. I felt I had held privilege to some sort of insider knowledge for years and I was a tad skeptical as I began reading.

As I waded through the essays, however, I was repeatedly struck by particular passages that seemed to spring wildly off the pages, as if to scream, "Oh my God! You, David Lacy, know that same exact feeling damned well, and you've never been able to express it that way!" Communal perspectives that so many will be able to relate to emerge early on in this collection, even as distinct stories provide remarkable insights, heartbreaking traumas, and ultimately some phenomenal coping mechanisms.

Themes of distorted self-perception, parental figures who shamed us into anguish, and unhealthy responses to weight gain or loss, appear and reappear throughout this important anthology. At the same time, each writer's account of his or her private battle reveals the infinite number of strategies people may employ to navigate through and even survive this pervasive sense of feeling out of place in their own skin.

Debra and I hope this book will become your own personal support group. Absorb these tales one at a time, in any order you find makes the most sense to you, and use them to realize you are not alone. My wish is that you discover your own passages leaping from the pages and screaming at you, and that you highlight or underline those passages (feel free to color and scribble all over this text!) or, better yet, type up or photocopy the ones from which you derive a sense of comfort, and paste them to the top of your mirror like a middle finger to the heartless looking glass that has no sense of empathy for the human being it reflects.

In Dancing at the Shame Prom: Sharing the Stories that Kept Us Small, iPinion contributors Amy Ferris and Hollye Dexter wrote in their own forward that they wanted "to shatter the stigma of that scary word shame and send this message to women (and men) everywhere: You are not alone – we are right there with you." We share their mission.

"Belly Shame: Stories From the Gut" is iPinion Syndicate's first book. We hope you'll consider this anthology a companion text in every sense of the word. These 12 writers are honored to remain by your side as you traverse the simultaneously universal and uniquely singular relationships with that thing that is at once defining of and irrelevant to your identity — your belly.

We just hope you have the guts to work through this with us.

Big Beauty and Belly Shame

DEBRA DeANGELO

I googled "belly shame" recently, and what popped up? A verse from Philippians and stories about pork bellies. No one has coined the term "belly shame" yet? How can this be, given that nearly every American female has it? Maybe we're so ashamed of our bellies, we can't even say the words out loud?

Just ask women how they feel about their bellies, and most will wrinkle their nose in discomfort. They won't even respond with words, and if they do, they're derogatory. We hate our bellies, to a pathological degree. Why? Because belly shame is drilled into us from childhood.

I was talking with a friend about bellies yesterday, and she told me about going to summer camp as a child. She was sitting in a two-piece bathing suit and another girl pointed to her and said, "Ewww — you have rolls. It was the first time I felt ashamed of my body. Before that, I didn't know anything was wrong with me."

She added another salient point: The girl who ridiculed her had already gotten the message that a normal, fleshy belly is disgusting.

My own belly shame began while reading a teen magazine. Sandwiched between a feature on Donny Osmond and a how-to piece on macrame was an article about weight, which declared: "An inch of pinch equals flab." I pinched. I was flabby times three! I was horrified! I was suddenly physically unacceptable!

I was 12.

And so it begins.

By the time girls become teens, if we succumb to Big Beauty, we've accepted that however we're shaped, it's wrong. And there's a product to fix that!

Except it doesn't.

And we buy it by the caseload anyway.

Ladies, how many times have you seen magazine headlines that scream, "Ban That Belly Fat"? You know why there are so many? Because they sell. It's not really about bellies. It's about bucks, and how many belly shaming rakes in.

More recently, round bottoms and ample thighs have become mainstream sexy, and I thank you, my sexy sisters of color, for raising awareness that beauty comes in a variety of shapes, colors, and sizes. Sadly, no one of any color has been able to do the same for bellies. Ghetto booty, yes. Ghetto belly, oh hell no.

I wonder if the source of belly hatred is evolutionary: Maybe our cavemen ancestors avoided thick-waisted females because they were likely already pregnant and therefore poor choices for mates. A tiny waist means fertile ground. A thick waist — maybe not. Maybe men are genetically predisposed to avoid thick-waisted women. Something to think about. Kinda makes sense. Those cavemen who got a rise for round-bellied women didn't spread their seed any further. They went the way of the pterodactyl.

As for belly fat itself, true too much isn't healthy. But I'm not talking about a 57-inch apple-shaped person on a path to heart disease. When I say "belly shame," I mean average, garden variety, normal American females with average, garden variety, normal American bellies.

Women stupidly — yes stupidly! — compare their normal bellies to the perfectly taut, flat abdomens of the professional anorexics on the fashion magazine covers and believe that unless their bellies look like that, they're fat. You know what? Most of those models don't have perfect bellies either. They're the creation of someone sitting at a computer, transforming women into his/her own idea of female perfection.

In other words, those women — those bellies — don't actually exist, except in a "Plato's Table" fashion.

Hmmm. "Plato's Belly."

Hint: It doesn't exist.

Belly shame is painful enough on its own, but it's exaggerated even more after we have babies. Except for a rare, lucky few, our bellies are never the same after we give birth. They're plumper. They sag. The muscles are stretched and no matter how many crunches we do, our abs never look the same as before. Some of us have caesarian scars. Most of us have stretch marks — and, a thousand crunches a day won't change that.

Most women look at their stretch marks and feel despair. The notion of wearing a bikini is abandoned, and we suddenly prefer sex with the lights out. We see flaws rather than the symbols of how our bellies got that way: by carrying and birthing the babies we love more than our next breath.

An interesting movement exploded onto social media via Instagram recently: "Love Your Lines." It's helping women to not only accept, but be proud of their stretch marks. Women are starting to push back against the "stretch marks = ugly" meme. If we can learn to "love our lines," could we also learn to love our bellies?

Mother's Day traditionally is the second Sunday in May. How about making every day Mother's Day, and celebrating it with some self-mothering and purging of our belly shame? Begin by replacing your negative thoughts and feelings with positive ones. First, stand in front of the mirror naked and just look at your belly. (I bet you're squirming already. How sad is that?) Cradle your belly, like the famous Gaia statue created by Oberon Zell, and for every negative thought you have, say to yourself — out loud, so your brain hears it — "Beautiful belly." Rinse and repeat.

If your belly shows the saggy, striped signs of having carried children, here's another mantra: "I love my kids." Recall your love for your children, really feel it in your heart, and transfer it to the visible signs of having carried them. Channel that pure, sweet love right onto your belly. Your scars. Your stretch marks. Feel the love there. Trust me, that infusion of self-love will feel infinitely more wonderful than your lifetime of belly shame.

We women still have some work to do. We've reclaimed our sexuality via birth control. We've made strides in equal rights, voting, education, employment, and finances. We've cleared these external hurdles, but still stumble over the internal ones — the ones that erode our self-esteem.

Let's reclaim our self-esteem, beginning with our bellies. Reject Big Beauty. Embrace your beautiful belly. It's fine just the way it is. Don't be the one who tells you otherwise.

A Middle Finger to the Lady in the Mirror

CAROLYN WYLER

"Mirror, mirror on the wall..."

I didn't need to finish my 15-20 times daily ritual — I knew how it would end. The lady staring back at me in the mirror would inevitably be laughing hysterically and pointing at my gut. Almost every time I walked by, she stood there mocking me.

Sometimes I try to ignore her, but in an attempt to pass her without an acknowledgement, I'd hear her calling to me.

"Hey — where are you going, Fatty?"

She would lure me in and I'd inevitably go stand by her, suck in my gut, and try to prove to her that I was not a fatty.

On more confident, fuck you days, I could walk by, flip her off and yell back, "Well, you try having four kids and be halfway between 50 and 60 and tell me if you can pull this off!" Those days, I'd see her smile back at me and apologetically say, "You are absolutely correct! You look fabulous!" (Those days, unfortunately, are few and far between).

I could put the blame for not having a perfect body on my four kids. B.C. (before children), my belly was pretty flat and I rarely had problems fitting into clothes. Now, 27 years A.C. (after children) I wiggle, squirm, and hold my breath to squeeze into a pair of jeans, and my belly has an ugly bulge.

Or, I could easily blame my belly shame on society. It perpetually places glamorous, way too thin women up on a pedestal as a model of what women should aspire to. I had never been and would never be that perfect specimen of a woman. That doesn't stop me from wanting to be a perfect specimen, however, and the image of my flabby gut in the mirror is just one of the constant reminders of what I'll never attain.

And of course there's always my mother, though at this point in my life, I'm not sure what good it does digging up that grave. Not that my mother, and certainly all mothers, don't deserve some of the credit/blame for our insecurities or upbringing. At some point in your adult life however, you need to take responsibility for your own thoughts and actions and move on.

When I was a child, religion was immensely important. As a teenager, an average week would consist of attending seven church services, saying at least twenty-one prayers and constantly being reminded that God, like a drone, is watching our every action. We lived, breathed and ate religion to the point that you'd think the mass consumption would make us all morbidly obese.

All eight of us (my parents, four brothers and one sister) though, were quite physically fit. We ate homegrown fruits and vegetables, and fresh eggs from the chickens we had in our back yard. We would grind wheat, which was made into whole wheat bread and breakfast cereal with low-fat powdered milk. There was no way we could gain weight on that regimen.

We certainly appeared to be the "perfect family." We probably could have auditioned and replaced the characters from "The Waltons," having only to change a few of the letters in the name.

I don't remember having very many fights in our family (my mom would have the final word and win them anyway, so what was the point?). We didn't cuss ("pissed" and "stupid" were among the list of swear words we were not allowed to use). We didn't smoke, didn't have a "recipe" (i.e. alcohol, as the Waltons had), didn't do drugs, skip school, steal, or cheat.

I never lied. (Well, except for that one time I told the school nurse that I felt sick because I didn't want to go outside in the Illinois 32-degree temperature for recess). I felt so much guilt after telling that lie that I didn't feel worthy to take the sacrament (blood and body of Christ) for one whole year. I would feel the pains and anguish in my gut every Sunday as the Sacrament was passed around, terrified my parents would notice and my horrible deed would be exposed. At that time, I concluded that it was probably more than a coincidence that "guilt" and gut for me, were only different because of two simple letters: a little (white) li.

Looking back on my childhood, I realize now that the only thing more important than religion was the need to appear as if we were the perfect family. Though we all looked really good on the outside, some of us were struggling with inner issues we couldn't confide to anyone who might bring down the image of our perfect family.

I was nicknamed "Sweet Sister" (much to the dismay of my older sister, who was affectionately called "Sour Power," but quite frankly, I admired her spunky, questioning attitude). I was more quiet and easygoing — a "holding in my needs and wants in order to keep everyone else happy" type of person.

Holding in all my emotions eventually caught up with me, ate up my gut, and burst out into a flood of emotions.

Toward the end of my mother's life, her memory began to fade. A couple years before she died, she came up to me to introduce herself. She was quite surprised at first that her last name was the same as mine and asked me if she was older than I. She finally recognized me as her daughter (the one child of hers who no longer goes to church). I'll always remember when she leaned over and whispered in my ear how pretty I looked.

I walk by the image in the mirror and suck in my gut, then turn back and flip her off.

Real Tummies Don't Have Six-Packs

CHRISTY SILLMAN

I have 11 scars on my belly: one Cesarean section scar, one seven-incher from an open appendectomy and bowel removal, four from my laparoscopic cholecystectomy, and five chest tube insertion sites... not to mention the stretch marks, roll of fat, fluid retention, and bloated gas. Underneath the skin is a whole other mess of gastrointestinal issues. I don't have a Victoria's Secret tummy, and I never will. It's the one part of my body of which I feel most ashamed.

As a young child, I constantly had children and adults asking me about my funny looking scars. I searched for bathing suits that would strategically hide the pits and dips from years of chest tubes. As a teenager, I even went so far as to have reconstructive plastic surgery while awake. I only made it through one of the four scar revisions because for some reason, the surgeon made me feel uncomfortable.

That same surgeon was arrested a few years later after raping his patients while unconscious on the operating table. I would have hated myself if vanity had led me to rape. I was so thankful I followed my gut and its perfectly fine scars out of that operating room.

I only remember one time when I was truly proud of my stomach and showed it off willingly: when I was pregnant. Being pregnant was a complete celebration. I was overcoming many odds in creating this precious life inside of me and my big belly was my trophy. My belly was something to gush over and rub, and I spent hours admiring it. I miss my pregnant belly, and the comfortable maternity clothes that came with it.

I hate my belly the most when I'm getting dressed in the morning. I've recently gained a few pounds, and I'm refusing to buy properly fitting clothes. Nothing makes you feel worse about your belly than trying to stuff it into your favorite pair of work slacks and attempting to avoid bending all day long. I spend my days dreaming of the moment I get to slip back into my pajama pants.

I've struggled through years with tummy troubles on the inside as well — paroxysmal lactose and gluten intolerance, acid reflux, gallbladder attacks, and general bloat from a GI system that's been cut apart and put back together again one too many times. I've been on many restricted diets and have watched my belly instantly swell from falling "off the wagon" and eating too much salty gluten. If I'm not disgusted by the outside of my belly, then I'm crippled by the inside.

How do we find love and acceptance of our bellies when there's so much pressure from society to look a certain way? We have to change the way we look at our own tummies. I think we start by feeding our tummies healthy food. A healthy tummy is a happy tummy. When I stick to a low-sodium, low-gluten, fresh produce diet, my tummy rewards me with happy feelings and clothes that fit comfortably. I'm also not going to beat myself up if I occasionally indulge in a delicious treat. What is life worth if you can't savor a Nutella croissant?

Ultimately, it's not about the six-pack, it's about the bowel movement.

If you ask a nurse her opinion on tummies, you're going to end up discussing poop. When your poop is unhealthy it's a sign that *you're* unhealthy. If you're having regular, soft, formed bowel movements then you're on the right track. Anything otherwise needs a serious diet evaluation.

Next, we must stop comparing our tummies to those in the media. Those tummies are *not real*. The men and women who have those rock-hard bellies are gym slaves who seriously limit their diets. It's a lot of work just to achieve an "ideal" look. Few people have the time to keep up with that, and it's time we stop beating ourselves up for not fitting the mold.

Today, when you're out in public, look at the tummies around you. *Real tummies.* They come in all different shapes and sizes. Real tummies are not chiseled by an artist or airbrushed into shapes that defy physics. Real tummies are squishy, jiggly, and sometimes tell a story.

I need to find pride in my tummy the way I did when I was pregnant. The scars that cover my tummy are a testament to my fighting spirit. The stretch marks are reminders that I risked it all to have my son. The swelling and bloating are reminders to stay heart-healthy. I must even be thankful for the layer of fat, as there was a time in my life when I was dangerously underweight from my heart working too hard. I'm so thankful my heart works well enough to keep fat around.

My belly imperfections tell my story. They make me who I am. They're not something to run from. I need to hug my belly tight, tell it I love it, and stop feeling ashamed. I am real.

Real people have flaws, and that's what makes us interesting.

I'm the Leader of SLOBS

DONALD SANDERS

I am not ashamed of my large belly. To prove it, I've decided to start my own fat belly cult. Only those with big bellies will be accepted into my cult, and the bigger the better. The modern world is practically making us fat. We have fats and sugars everywhere in our society and most of us sit around all day stressing out. It's only natural that we have big bellies.

In my new society, there will be an explosion of obesity. Being overweight is not enough, because if you are not obese, your chance of having Type 2 diabetes is cut in half. It's only natural that humans are obese. This one amazing fact has been proven over and over despite what the government and the mass media have been telling us.

To the government we're just so many sheep and cattle to be jammed into trucks and vans. The media tells us that slim is healthier. Do not believe this, because it's a ploy to keep you skinny so more of us will fit into each prison cell. They tell us that slim is healthier and better for us. They say thin people are happier. Ha. Have you ever seen a jolly skinny guy? Hell no!

As you will see, gaining weight to reach obesity is a simple matter of eating more and exercising less. Gyms, jogging, swimming, and hiking are totally unsuited for human beings. All of these things are designed to increase your stress levels and keep your food consumption levels to a minimum. Skinny people are easier to manage, and the government knows that skinny people eat less than happy fat people.

Our world is noisy, crowded, and contaminated, so we all live in a hostile environment that is dangerous to our health. We are told to consume plant based unsaturated and polyunsaturated fats instead of trans-fatty acids that are most supportive of health. To reach the desired level of obesity it is recommended that we consume 12 fluid ounces of trans-fat daily.

My cult, "Sexy Loyal Obese Brothers and Sisters" (SLOBS), will have members with a zealous and unquestioning commitment to their leader: ME. I see to it that meal portions do not remain stable but increase in portion on a daily basis. Cookies, pasta, and ice cream portions will stagger to a level seven times higher every month. As leader of the SLOBS, my word is taken as truth, as the law, and there is no questioning or dissent that will go unpunished.

There will be mind-altering practices such as meditation, chanting, speaking in tongues, denunciation sessions, and debilitating work routines that will be used in excess and serve to suppress doubts about the group and its leader. The group recognizes that I'm on a mission to save humanity from itself. A person with a big belly is a happy person.

Peer pressure and subtle forms of persuasion will help you focus on your obesity goals. Failure is not an option because, "If you are skinny, you don't get a penny!" (That's one of my famous quotes.) The most loyal members (the "true believers") feel there can be no life outside the fold of the group. In the not so distant future I can envision camps where thin people will no longer be a threat to my SLOBS.

A true SLOBS member will no longer feel ashamed of his/her big belly because in a perfect world, a big belly is a happy belly. Join SLOBS today!

Embrace the Belly

HANNAH SULLIVAN

There are people out there who want you to feel ashamed and embarrassed of your belly. Newsflash — I don't need anyone to make me feel that way because I can do that all on my own. Trust me, when my muffin top becomes a full-on soufflé — I'm feeling it.

There are a few things I've learned to deal with being someone who has a belly. Sometimes they aren't even belly related problems, but I know we all experience them.

1. Chub rub. Being someone who has some extra chub, I get what's called "chub rub." You know when you're wearing shorts or a dress and your thighs rub together, and you get some discomfort where they touch? Maybe even get a rash? I have solved this problem with deodorant. You rub a little on each thigh and you're good to go! Don't knock it until you try it!

2. Wearing holes into your favorite jeans. The chub strikes again! There's no cure for this kind of chub rub, unfortunately (that I know of). I can't tell you how many holes I've burned into the crotch of my jeans from my thighs scraping together all day. It's always the best pair too. Another sacrifice to the chubby thigh goddesses.

3. Cardigans and "fat jackets." I know the name isn't flattering, but it's what I jokingly call jackets and sweaters I wear over tank tops and dresses. I don't think I have the fattest arms I've ever seen, but covering them up sometimes on those not-so-confident-days makes me feel a little bit better. Most of my wardrobe consists of cardigans and flowy things, and I can't decide if I do it consciously to cover up or because I actually just like the style. Either way — I'm okay with this.

4. The ole hair elastic around the pant button routine. I heard about this trick from someone talking about how to keep wearing normal jeans once your pregnant belly starts coming in. I, however, use this trick when my food baby is coming in. It's not noticeable at all! I promise! I've done this trick a few times and have even worn T-shirts with it. If you feel uncomfortable, wear a belt to cover it. I

know this trick is pretty lame, but if you're bloated and need a quick fix, this is for you.

5. Strut. This isn't a problem to overcome — it's how to overcome your problems. If I'm having a bad day and all I feel like doing is eating or I feel like everyone is silently judging me, I strut. I put on my favorite songs, hold my head up high, and just feel the confidence flow through me. You don't need reassurance from anyone else but you to feel good. Even if you don't feel confident, just fake it! I do this all the time. I tell myself I look damn good, and I start to feel good.

The body acceptance movement is now louder than the body shame movement. The ones who try to shout louder about our bellies cannot win. Let their comments roll right off of you (no pun intended) and remember that you only have one body so, love it for all it's worth because you are worth it! If you are trying to change your body, don't give up! You can't change in a day. We all have off days, cheat days, and good days. Not everyone has the same body type so don't think everyone needs to be a size 2. I will never be a size 2 and that's okay.

Don't let the belly hold you back! Embrace it!

My Belly, My Self

JUDITH NEWTON

I remember a photograph of me at 8 years old. I'm standing in a lake, wearing a one-piece bathing suit, my belly protruding so far in its dark, latex sack that I look like I'm pregnant. My mother, despite my tearful objections, insisted on pasting that picture into the family album, and there I was — pinned for eternity it seemed — like an engorged insect for everyone to see.

For most of my childhood and adolescence, I regarded that photo with a shame that squeezed my insides so tight that I felt like fainting. It was not just that I and my belly were fat and that fatness was scorned, it was that my extended stomach had ties to another, deeper, source of humiliation — a feeling that there was something horrifying about me, something I could never divulge.

I'd arrived at this sense of self-horror four years before when my mother broke into tears at the news — delivered by a neighbor girl's mother — that I had "played doctor" with the boy down the street.

"I thought you were a good little girl," my mother sobbed, as if her world were breaking apart. But it was my world that shattered.

Anxious already at four years old because my mother maintained an unmotherly distance from me, angry at her, but always striving for her approval, I ceased, in that moment, to exist. I would spend much of my later life trying to recover that identity, trying to become the "good little girl" that I no longer thought I was, and I would internalize my mother's grief and shock into a conviction so paralyzing that I felt turned to stone: There was something shameful about me, a thing that must be hidden at all costs.

And so, I began to overeat. I ate because cooking and baking were my mother's most consistent form of nurturing and because my consumption of her apple pies and oatmeal cookies felt like a form of familial connection. I ate to take away the pain. And before long, living on meat, potatoes and sweets (largely composed of Crisco and sugar) I put on weight. As my belly bulged, it became, on some barely conscious level, a shameful symbol of my suffering and a reminder of the terrible thing about me that had first prompted me to say yes to my mother's Crackerjack and three kinds of fudge.

And so it went, until a bout of measles in the eighth grade caused me to lose a lot of weight and rescued me, momentarily, from the physical engorgement of my stomach. Saved at last. I was beside myself with relief. But even then, and even when I deliberately lost more weight, while safely away from home doing undergrad and graduate studies, that stomach, and the reasons for its origin, haunted me. Although my midsection grew concave in the 1960s, hipbones protruding, the ghost of my former belly remained—in a wrinkled circle of skin that looked like an empty, useless pouch.

In the '70s, I married and started my first job, constantly dieting to keep that belly in control, frequently begging my young husband to evaluate my figure. He looked at the circle of skin, white and sagging like a deflated moon.

"You should try to do something about that," he offered.

I thought so, too. But what could I do? The more I lost, the more skin hung down. Plastic surgery in the 1970s was still so exotic that I never considered it. Never mind that I couldn't have afforded it anyway.

Fast-forward to the middle '80s. After many years of psychotherapy, I felt grounded and grown up enough to have my own child and to become pregnant at last. It was the sole period of my life when I was happy about my stomach. I looked pregnant because I was, and my second husband and I took a series of pictures to document my belly's progress. I was giddy with happiness, and though my doctor scolded me for gaining weight too fast, I didn't care. I was having a baby whom I planned to shower with all the love and attention that had been absent from my childhood. When my daughter was born, I was reborn with her.

I wish I could say that my pregnancy changed everything forever. But it didn't. Although caring for my daughter became a lifelong joy, in times of stress and loss, I still had bouts of depression, which I've recently learned are now inscribed in my DNA. The 4-year-old girl, no longer shameful but still fragile with respect to her identity, made occasional reappearances, and the medications with which I was treated in the 1990s made me gain weight, occasionally restoring a minor version of the belly in that hated photograph.

Even when I dieted, moreover, I couldn't escape the past. My pregnancy had enlarged the mass of hanging skin. Like my childhood demons, my belly had never fully been erased. I learned to live with the demons. I imagine many of us do. But the belly? It was physical, it was concrete, and there was always the alluring possibility of alteration.

I'm at an age now when most women I know well have bellies, even when age has otherwise worn them to bone and sinews. It's a comfort to be in their company. I'm also at an age of new defiance, officially old, but refusing "to go gently into that good night." The poem I loved in the 1980s, "When I Am an Old Woman, I Shall Wear Purple," now applies to me. And maybe because of that defiance, I'm still engaged in thinking about my belly. If I could afford it, honestly, I'd get the surgery. I could be less straightforward and say I wouldn't, but I no longer need to pose as so "good" a little girl.

Last fall, ironically enough, I was diagnosed with a stomach condition that had gone unchecked for many years, and once my naturopath put me on a diet excluding everything in the universe but vegetables and protein, the wrinkled moon stomach reappeared. I infinitely prefer it to the protruding belly in the latex sack, and maybe I can even learn to like it. Maybe not. But, at least, there's been some closure about the photograph that haunted me. When my mother died, I became the keeper of the family album. The first thing I did when I got my hands on it was to take that picture out and tear it up.

Fat Guy Brain

TOM McMASTERS-STONE

Belly shame, body shame... it's the same thing, *n'est pas*?

When did it start for me? At childbirth, chronologically, but practically, as soon as I could understand the comments, and even the hidden meaning in "cute" or "healthy" or "future football player."

Methinks that firstborn children are too often steered in this direction. Baby cries, and the answer is sticking a bottle or food in their mouths.

As I grew up, it manifested itself in many ways as I trudged along. When my neighborhood peers in Upstate New York shunned me and picked on me, I would go home and come back bearing snacks or treats. In elementary school, I became the class clown. There's nothing like humor to mask the pain. About this time, I also became a voracious reader. Escapism — into history, into the wilderness, into brotherhoods, or to happily-ever-after.

To their credit and love, none of my dozens and dozens of cousins participated in picking on me. There were limits to what they'd tolerate, too. One jumped up and broke the maple pointer in half when Sister St. Andrew was beating me, describing her as a "battle-axe" while he did. The best three-day vacation ever!

I was also ostracized when I entered junior high and high school — except that now I was interested in girls. The problem was that not only did they ridicule me, they made fun of the girls, too. In high school, no Freshman Dances, no Sophomore Hops, no Junior Proms, or Senior Balls — and no Homecomings. Several times, some of my female friends told me they need somebody "just like me." I was standing there, in front of them, unattached. I guess they wanted a thinner version of me. Finally, I got a girlfriend as a senior. She was a freshman, and it took some work.

I didn't get my driver's license until I was 18. They had turned me into an amoeba, and I was afraid. Even though things started turning around when I became a very talented soccer player in my sophomore year, it was a slow process — and is ongoing to this day.

Yes, to this day.

No amount of educational achievement, career success, or political accomplishments has made much of a dent.

Eight years ago, I gave up and had gastric bypass surgery. At 5'11", I sit here hovering at 220 pounds — down over 150 pounds.

Epiphany? Armageddon?

Nope.

The fat guy brain is still in place.

Collateral damage? Sure. Most significantly, I cannot tell you what I meant to my first wife, or what I mean to my second wife, my children, my grandchildren, or my niece and nephews. No idea. To my friends either. I am not feeling sorry for myself, but it is a tragedy.

Yes, I still feel awkward going around with my shirt off.

The love of my life, who has some parallel history, doesn't get the fat guy brain — not really.
I got back from a Vegas trip awhile back, and told her I got hit on several times. Her reply was "Anybody can get laid in Vegas."

More recently, I told her about a few times I'd been hit on, and she got angry, thinking I was trying to make her jealous. Sadly, I quietly told her, "No, I was just sharing my joy with you." Historically, she and I don't play jealousy games. I will just celebrate those occasions quietly and to myself from now on. I don't play the macho, bragging game.

We met some folks at a social event a week ago, and one of the women we met — a good-looking 40-something — showed up at the ranch the next day, riding her horse. A couple of the guys suggested she come by because she had an interest in me. In my mind, however, I was at the bottom of her list.

Also, to this day, I don't like having my picture taken, and there were only a handful of them along the way that I actually liked. Rarely does my profile on Facebook or Twitter include a picture of me.

Did this contribute to the severe childhood PTSD I've been recently diagnosed with? Undoubtedly, it is a big part of it. Vertical PTSD *and* Horizontal PTSD. Or perhaps Missionary PTSD? Bwahahaha!

I finished Diana Gabaldon's "Outlander" series recently. When I began it, my wife suggested that I might not want to read it. I thought that a little odd at the time, but I quickly understood why: the love story of lifetime kindred spirits, unable to keep their minds or hands off one another for very long. I loved the series. Until life interfered, as life often does, I experienced that kind of love story for a few years. I may never get it back, or experience it again. I'm okay with that, as some people never get to experience it at all.

But I do miss it horribly.

Thick Vanilla Shame

KATHY BROTHERTON

I was 9 years old when I became ashamed of my body.

Summer vacations in Connecticut every year to visit my dad was the norm of my childhood. My dad would spend two weeks creating magic. We would go to amusement parks, stuff ourselves with cotton candy, ride every ride, play every game. We would visit the Bronx Zoo, ride the camels and elephants. Our evenings were filled with eating steak and shrimp, chasing fireflies at dusk. It was the happiest two weeks of the year.

My dad's girlfriend asked me if I wanted to come with her to McDonald's to get breakfast for the four of us. I jumped at the opportunity to ride in the front seat of Kim's sports car. I felt adult, important. Kim spoke to me like she valued my opinions.

As we stood in line at McDonald's, I sheepishly looked over to Kim and asked her if I could have a vanilla milkshake. Without the slightest bit of hesitation, she went out of her way to put a smile on my face.

"Of course you can have a milkshake!"

It was vanilla, it was thick. I quietly sipped slowly at the straw, drinking it steadily was we drove back to my father's apartment.

My father was clearly annoyed as we came through the door with the bags of food. A lit cigarette hung from his mouth as he removed dishes from the dish drain and angrily slammed them on the counter. His head turned in almost slow motion as his gaze landed upon the cup in my hand. I could see the color creep up his neck straight to the top of his head. He was as red as the tomatoes that grew outside his screen door in ceramic pots.

"What the hell is that?" he demanded of Kim.

The ash dropped from his cigarette, hitting the clean floor. For every ounce of color that my father's face gained, Kim's face had lost. She was white, her face devoid of any emotion, her tone clearly exhibiting confusion.

"It is a milkshake."

The dish in his hand shattered against the wall as my father burst into a raging tirade.

"A milkshake? Do you want to be fat like your mother and her entire family? What's next? Shoving cupcakes in your mouth like a little pig? No daughter of mine is going to be fat!"

His fury was aimed at me. It felt never-ending.

I felt my cheeks flush hot as the cup slipped from my hand in fear. Wetting my pants was the icing on the cake that capped off the fear, anger, humiliation I felt in that moment. I wanted to tear his eyes out for saying hurtful words about my mother. I wanted to run and hide from his disapproval. I wanted the floor, now covered in speckled white dots of the ice cream goodness, to swallow me alive.

I ran full speed two doors down to my great-grandmother. I was hysterical; I couldn't get my breath to control the tears. I climbed up into her lap like a little monkey. She consoled me until she could extract the story.

She let him have it that day. She also demanded he bring my suitcase to her house. I would be staying with her for the remainder of the vacation. That night, after my bath, I stood in the mirror looking at my childlike body. I pulled at the skin that surrounded my stomach. I saw it as fat. Horrible rippling fat that was going to eat me alive was starving me of my father's love.

I became fixated on my body that day. Heading into puberty it got significantly worse. Trips to Connecticut were no longer the magical wonderland they had once been. I would stop eating weeks before it was time to go, starving off anything that could be construed as the slightest bit of fat. I then learned to purge to get my mother off my back about eating.

The bulimic episodes came and went through my teens. It got especially bad my senior year of high school. A friend informed my guidance counselor, who thought it would be a great idea to call my dad.

Boy was she wrong.

"She is a rebellious child vying for attention any way that she can get it. I cook every night. She eats every night, end of story."

He stomped out.

I sat there in the meeting tuning out my father's criticism. I just shrugged.

"He's right," I whispered. "I don't throw up."

My counselor took me by the arm and led me up to her office.

"I'm sorry that I didn't listen when you said calling your father would make this worse. I don't need his permission to help you — you're 18 years old."

My mouth opened and closed slowly. I pressed my face against the cool Formica of her desk and let the tears flow.

I went for some treatment, which didn't last. I didn't perceive *how* I controlled my weight as a problem. I kept purging until I was 19 years old. It was seeing a tiny grain of rice on an ultrasound with a tiny blip of a heartbeat that stopped the compulsion to purge.

"Eat or she has no chance," the doctor informed me.

I went on to have three beautiful, healthy children, gaining more belly fat with each child. I was given a diagnosis of Polycystic Ovary Syndrome. My belly fat will lead to diabetes and worse if I do not get it under control immediately. I'm currently on a low carbohydrate, gluten-free diet with a cocktail of meds to shock my body out of insulin resistance.

While the excessive fat on my body is a dangerous health risk, it's no longer a mental health risk. I raised my children — both my daughter and two sons — to love their bodies, embrace who they are and always be the best you that you can be. Whoever that is, I love endlessly without judgment. I let the prejudices of my childhood form me into the supportive, non-judgmental parent that I became.

In the interim, I think I'll have a thick sugar-free coconut milk vanilla milkshake, large and foamy. This time I'll drink every last sip to the bottom of the cup.

Shame Happens When Others Decide Our Worth

KATHIE YOUNT

When will we learn to respect everyone?

When I think of the day that time divided into two parts for me and rehear what my son heard in the hour before his death — "fat white boy," among other shaming insults — my heart has difficulty remembering how to beat.

My son was neither a boy, nor fat, although he was white.

Throughout most of his life, he was usually regarded as having a handsome physique and every refining grace of character without the tragic flaw of conceit. But like many of us, my son had experienced a benign period of chubbiness during his elementary school years, which he outgrew because, like most of us, Dylan Yount did not want to be "fat."

Yet if Dylan could speak now about the last photo taken of him alive, he would definitely have been the first to point out that he had weighed more than he had any other time of his life. He would also have pointed out the situational irony — with a self-deprecating laugh, perhaps — that he had died on Fat Tuesday 2010.

The last picture of him is unflattering. The very last ones of him are even worse, but maybe they always are by definition and the bygone time of photographic aperture after we are no longer alive inside our bodies. Nevertheless, the last live images of him standing on the little ledge promontory above the former Forever 21 store is destined for inclusion in social psychology textbooks and went viral back in February 2010. Today, it continues to be a flashpoint in the lugubrious legal literature that documents Kathy Yount et al. v. City and County of San Francisco et al.

It resonated enough that one of the 311 city attorneys for San Francisco wrote about the last "shape" of his earthly body posture, complaining that Dylan should "appear more troubled." Ten words later, her word choice – "the weight of his decision" – leaves me weak, for I firmly believe her choice of the word "weight" was judgmental whether she used it intentionally or subconsciously.

Why Deputy City Attorney Elizabeth Pederson seems to hate the Younts is beyond me, but she would not make eye contact with me inside the court chambers of the First District Court of Appeal on August 20, 2015, for Oral Arguments in Yount v. CCSF even though I could see her in my peripheral vision occasionally looking at me. Each time I'd turn to look directly into her eyes, she would deliberately look away. While I would use another word to describe Lady Elizabeth, Dylan would have used "hot," and I smile remembering how much fun he was.

I feel as if I have given her credit where it is due, which is not much. She was accurate to say that Dylan was "standing with a bent knee and a hand on his hip," just as Justice Needham reiterated that same assessment during Oral Arguments. Justice Needham added, though, that this was an unfortunate circumstance because "we lost a life," and that he noticed Dylan "wasn't engaging." And this is true as well. Victims of suicide baiting do not engage with those encouraging them to kill themselves. They absorb. They are silent, and their silence demonstrates their anxiety. While Elizabeth tried to paint Dylan's behavior before his death as "casual," she misses or ignores the point. His behavior was causal.

In fact, the cause and effective relationship is exactly what happens in a suicide baiting. Victims feel shame, which is the predominate feature of all psychological disorders. Shame always directs us to destructive behavior, which we either internalize or externalize.

Shame is all about making someone feel unworthy, disconnected, or "less" than others. Shame is the most powerful weapon in the arsenal mean people use to destroy someone else's sense of who they are. Shame is a condition, not an emotion. It is what we feel when others decide we are defective or stupid.

"Fool" and "fat," among other insults, are words my beautiful son heard from the crowd and that crowd's 24 managing San Francisco police officers who all skyrocketed into judgmental overdrive in Hallidie Plaza, San Francisco, on 2-16-10: "He's not going to jump – he's *high*!"

Dylan heard, mentally and physically, "You are unworthy. Your heart has no further reason to beat. Suicide will be the only decision you can never regret. Only the living can feel regret."

"If you're going to do the shit, do the shit."

"JUMP!"

A suicide baiting is the moral equivalent of kicking a man who is already down. In a suicide baiting, the victim always "feeds" off the crowd.

Sometimes people who need help look like people who don't. A man standing on a ledge always needs help. Would the crowd – and the SFPD – have behaved differently if the man on the ledge had been Robin Williams?

Beyond Belly Shame

KELVIN WADE

Belly shame? Try body shame.

I was at a loss when tasked to write about "belly shame." Since when do men have belly shame? It's women who ask, "Does this dress make my ass look like a rhino's?" not men. I've never known a woman who didn't have anxiety over her hips, thighs and especially, belly. It didn't matter if the woman was thin and athletic, she could always find that flaw. Meanwhile, a man can be balding with crooked teeth, wearing tattered tighty-whities, with his asscrack showing and a gut hanging out from under his T-shirt, and look in the mirror and think he's a stud.

"Oh yeah, the ladies want me!"

What has evolution done to us?

Look, I'm a fat man. I was probably 50 pounds at birth and it kept going from there. Many of my childhood memories revolve around the comfort of food. Peanut butter and jelly sandwiches at daycare. Ordering crinkle cut French fries at the swimming pool. A Smithfield ham on the Sunday dinner table.

Little boys aren't cognizant of body image at 7 years old. I did the same things as other kids my age. We played kickball and football, rode bikes and even had foot races. In a lot of ways, I was just like any other kid. But as I got older, I saw that clothes that fit me were harder to come by.

At school, I was that fat kid picked last for sports. While I could kick a ball a mile or knock a softball into the outfield, what would've been a homerun for other kids was just a double for me. For Halloween, since I couldn't fit into a store-bought costume, my mother had me wear black leotards, a black cape and mask and carry a toy sword. I was supposed to be Zorro but I looked like a fat, armed ballerina.

So, growing up, I didn't have "belly shame." I had body shame. I was bashful. Wherever I was, the thing I felt like doing was blending into the background. Anything to not be noticed. I didn't want to stand out in a crowd because I knew I'd be standing out for all the wrong reasons.

For years, I never even saw myself as a body. It was easier just to deny that I was a hippopotamus and focus on the two things I had at my disposal: my charm and my intellect. I thought maybe if I could dazzle people they wouldn't notice my excessively spherical shape. Sometimes it worked but often it didn't.

Feeling bad about one's body ironically fuels the pernicious cycle of overeating. Being teased by kids at school, my brothers or my father (who often referred to me as "Fatso Freddy") didn't send me to the treadmill to lose weight. It sent me to the refrigerator to drown my sorrows in Coca-Cola and Pop-Tarts.

My poor body image paralyzed me. It dictated where I went, what I did and whom I met. I'll never forget being at this club with some friends and there was this thick girl in a leather skirt eyeballing me all night. She was cute. Even when we left the club, she followed us out, still looking at me as we were figuring out what to do with the rest of the evening. Her eyes said, "Talk to me," and that scared fat voice in my head said, "Maybe she's looking at someone behind you. If you go up and talk to her, she might reject you." I never got to find out.

That poor body image made me reckless. I discovered that in addition to food, I had a taste for drugs and alcohol. My older siblings' friends became my friends. They welcomed another Wade partyer with open arms. Being able to brew with the big boys impressed them and I found acceptance in that identity. Liquor, malt liquor, weed, crosstops, mushrooms. I was down for whatever. Trying crack cocaine with one of my brothers or snorting blow before heading into a Prince concert was fine with me. Being intoxicated made me feel like a whole different person.

When NWA and gangsta rap blew up in the late '80s and early '90s I found a new identity. Wannabe thug. Me and my friends went everyone packin'. We didn't give a fuck. Having that hardcore identity made me feel like somebody. I wasn't this timid obese guy with body shame. I did so many dangerous crazy things and the reason was simple: I didn't care if I lived or died. I made up for a lot of my inhibition by jumping into whatever I could find. Being a fake extrovert made me seem extroverted. It made me seem confident when in reality, my psyche was a mess.

My relationships with women were disastrous. Part of the reason was that they never seemed to be with me for me. Being cheated on and dumped added to my wretched self-image.

As an adult, I combated my self-loathing by doing something most fat people avoid: taking pictures of myself. My friends and I would videotape us hanging out and partying. I started the selfie-thing back in the '80s, taking tons of pictures of myself, desensitizing myself to my appearance. It helped. I got used to seeing myself and it helped me accept my body more, as gelatinous and blubbery as it was.

A big setback was developing lymphedema. Lymph fluid doesn't circulate normally throughout my body and instead, pools in my legs. Doctors aren't sure whether I damaged my lymph system or was born with it. My left leg has swollen tremendously and it has been a cause of shame because it's something I can't hide. Lymphedema is treatable but not curable, and the protein-rich fluid is ripe for infection. Since I have Stage III lymphedema, the worst kind, over the past 13 years I've been hospitalized more than a dozen times and have had dozens of outbreaks of cellulitis, a serious bacterial skin infection. I've been hospitalized in the ICU twice, the first time with renal failure due to a medication I was taking and the second time, a life-threatening bout with sepsis.

Those events prompted me to get off my ass and write my first two books of short stories, "Morsels: Twisted Tales of Life and Death Vol. I and II." In many ways, despite their weirdness, the stories are autobiographical. Especially the story "Freakshow," which is about acceptance.

No longer did I feel I had to be someone I wasn't. Long gone was the wannabe thug or the hardcore partyer. I'd settled down with a wonderful woman I'd met online who loved everything about me.

But the catalyst for change came a few years ago while listening to Hawaiian singer Israel "Iz" Kamakawiwo'ole's rendition of "Somewhere over the Rainbow/What a Wonderful World." It's a beautiful song with his melodic voice and ukulele. I'd heard the song over the years but never knew who sang it. When I googled him, I learned a lot of great things about him. However, the thing that struck me most was that he was a morbidly obese man who once weighed over 700 pounds and died at age 38.

His early death just flipped a switch in my head. Cue the theme from "Rocky." I went to my doctor with a bold medical plan to combat my recurring infections. I had to argue with my doctors to get them to agree with a plan I hoped would dramatically reduce my illnesses and hospital stays. Second, I joined Weight Watchers and attended weekly meetings. Instead of feeding off of fast food, I fed off the encouragement of my fellow members. I also started pumping iron. I've had some success in the past two years. No, I'm nowhere near thin. Pardon my French, but I typically tell people that I've went from being a fat fuck to a fat bastard. I don't have before and after pictures. I have "before" and "way before." Plus, I've gone from getting sick every six weeks with multiple hospitalizations a year to not having been hospitalized in two years. The medication regimen I fought for has worked beyond my wildest dreams.

Since then, I've dropped over 225 pounds. My blood pressure is 120/88, glucose is 90, and cholesterol is completely normal. People tell me I should buy new clothes because my clothes are too big and I blow them off. I've never worn clothes that were too big in my life. Let me enjoy it.

Even better is the fact that I'm more mentally healthy. "Live free. Fear nothing" has become my motto. I don't let body image dictate what I can do and what I can't.

I'm still obese. For someone who didn't know how I was, they'd be unimpressed looking at me. But I'm impressed. I know what I've done and the results I've obtained. I'm never going to look like Channing Tatum but that's okay. He's never going to be able to write like me.

Ready for the Beach

TRACEY YOKAS

A year and a half ago, I took a vacation to Hawaii with my husband and our daughter Olivia, and I did not swim. I walked into the warm beautiful blue Pacific Ocean up to my knees, stayed for one minute, then sat back down and covered up with a towel. I was embarrassed by the large size of my body, and certain that my family was equally embarrassed by me. I sat in my little beach chair — my bathing suit digging uncomfortably into my flesh — and smiled and pretended to be happy just to be there. It's hard to be happy when your self-esteem is as variable as the number on a scale.

When we decided to return again this year, I made a promise to myself that this time would be different. This time, regardless of my size, I would get all the way into the water. I promised myself that I would swim with my daughter. I promised myself that I would frolic, float and flip. I wanted to snorkel. I wanted my daughter to lift up her wet, sparkly masked head and see me, nearby, marveling with her at the colorful fish swimming beneath us. I wanted to stop letting the size of my body control the size of my life. So when I packed for this trip, I grabbed my old swimsuit out of the dresser drawer and threw it in my suitcase. I hoped it would fit.

Now here I am, standing in this condo's tiny bathroom, filled with dread that I won't be able to keep the promise I made to myself. I should have gone to Macy's Plus Size department and gotten a new suit, but that would have meant accepting that I have yet again grown larger. Instead, I told myself over and over, "It'll be fine. You haven't gained that much more weight." Now I have no choice. I have to make the old suit work.

I peel off my pajamas and already know how easy the lie will drip from my tongue should I need it, how the words I've had a lifetime to perfect will perch like dew on the edge of a petal.

"No, you go ahead to the beach. You know how sensitive my skin is. I'll be along in a while."

The suit is a two-piece, and I guide each foot through one of the bottom's leg holes and pull it up into place. So far, so good; it's tight but workable. The design of the top — the material long like a corset instead of short like a bra — requires me to pull it down over my head and into place. I get it right below my armpits when I hit a snag. Uh oh. The material bunches up and I can barely move it. It's really tight. I tug and shimmy and hop in place, hoping gravity will help me out. It doesn't. I'm sweating, which does not help, not one little bit. I'm stuck in this unattractive position — half naked with my too-small bathing suit top stuck at the approximate level of my armpits, performing a maneuver that looks like a demented version of the Funky Chicken — when I look down and see my bulging stomach. I fucking hate you, I think before I know I'm thinking it.

I can see the faded stretch marks that cover my stomach's surface area and remember the last time I stared at myself in the mirror, shocked by how much the stretch marks' raggedy, curved appearance reminded me of the shape of a Bloomin' Onion. I see the doughy flesh, no visible hint of ab muscle, let alone a six-pack. I see the horizontal red lines where my extra skin folds in when I sit down. And I see how much more skin I can pinch than one inch — at least three or four. Gross. Before I can stop it, my mental floodgate opens and waves of unkind thoughts crash upon me — thoughts I've worked to keep at bay for a long time.

Fat ass.

Loser.

You're worthless and disgusting.

You should be ashamed of yourself.

And I am. I'm drowning under this wave of criticism when it hits me that I will not let the last three years of my life be a total waste. I will not let these thoughts take me down. I have said that I love myself and my body as I am, and I will not let that be a lie.

Three years ago, my life was hell, and so was my daughter's. Olivia was diagnosed with an eating disorder and severe depression. She was 13. She woke up one day and decided that she was fat and disgusting, that she was ugly and worthless. She decided that she didn't deserve to live. At first, she coped with this pain by abusing food. She binged and purged or ate nothing at all. She lost 20 pounds in two months.

A little while later, she discovered that blood-letting with razor blades or whatever sharp object she could find was a far more effective coping mechanism than food to deal with her sadness, despair and rage. Instead of standing outside her bathroom door listening to her vomit, I found razor blades, broken glass and serrated knives hidden all over her bedroom: behind books in her bookcase, mixed in with her stuffed animals and nestled next to a plastic mood ring inside her ballerina jewelry box. I found her blood all over the place, too: dripped onto the floor in her bathroom, soaked into the sheets of her bed and running out of her arms. We screamed at each other. We ranted and raved. I begged and pleaded for her to stop cutting herself. She refused and said, "It's so cool to watch my blood pump through my veins." I called 911. She spent weeks on hospital psych wards and months in residential treatment because I could not keep her safe in her own home. I was confronted by the reality that every dream I had dreamt for her might be replaced by a life of revolving doors of inadequate care or, ultimately, by her death. I pondered if I would kill myself if she killed herself first. I was certain there was no bottom to the pit of grief and suffering we'd fallen into.

What I didn't know about how to help my daughter navigate this horror was enough to fill every volume of the Encyclopedia Britannica. The rational part of my brain whispered in my ear kind words about the genetics of mental illness and nature versus nurture. The rational part read and learned and problem solved at the speed of light. It tried to stay one step ahead by being diligent and taking care of business. But nothing worked to make Olivia get better.

What the irrational part of my brain — the seductive and believable part — knew about why Olivia was sick was far simpler: Whatever had gone wrong was my fault. I had failed her. To compensate for my inadequacies and to cope, I ate. As Olivia got smaller, I got larger. Much larger. My giant belly came to represent not only my failure as a person, but also as a mother. What's more fundamental to mothering than how we nourish our children? And how we nourish ourselves? I knew I should model good habits but eating was still the only place I found solace. Eating has always been the place I found solace.

When I was Olivia's age, I was already 35 pounds overweight. I prayed with all my might to be tall and beautiful with big boobs and a tiny waist. I knew that possessing these body characteristics would somehow solve my problems, even if I didn't really understand how or what my problems were. I longed to look like someone else, longed, I think, to be someone else – specifically, Lynda Carter from Wonder Woman or Jaclyn Smith from Charlie's Angels. I looked at those TV celebrities and at the popular kids in school and saw only what was different about me: my too big belly. I understood that it made me less of a person. My stomach became the physical manifestation of my belief in my inability to measure up, of my desire to be accepted, of my shame and of my longing to be loved unconditionally. A vicious lifelong cycle of battling my weight was born.

I dealt with my pain by overeating. My parents dealt with my overeating by doing what they thought was best and putting me on a diet. They loved me, but the message got reinforced: I was not good enough. The more I ate, the more ashamed I felt and the more ashamed I felt, the more I ate. My shame lodged in my belly and stayed there, growing even bigger and stronger by feeding off Ho-Hos and crumb coffee cake. Oh, and ice cream. My dad loved to take me to Dairy Queen for cones, and I loved anything that involved my dad.

The grievous problem with shame is this: Its power knows no boundaries. My shame about my body wasn't only confined to my body. On occasion, my shame spilled over and contaminated my feelings about my daughter's body, as well. I heard accusations all around me — when her pediatrician said that Olivia did, in fact, need to lose some weight or another mother rolled her eyes as Olivia gobbled up a snack at a party. The accusations caused me to second-guess decisions I'd made for my daughter that were different than the ones my parents had made for me regarding food and dieting. My second-guessing fed my harsh judgment — of me and of Olivia. Inside, I seethed against the world for making my daughter feel less than, against myself for failing to measure up, but also — utterly irrationally — against my pure and beautiful daughter herself for putting me in the indefensible position of not ending up with a better outcome than I had. The feeling was so primal and so deep that I often wondered if shame is genetically encoded into our DNA. How else would Olivia come to describe herself out loud using the exact same words I'd only thought privately about myself? In the future, I won't be surprised at all when science proves that shame links back to the very first caveman hunter who tried and failed to club his first beast.

Ten months into the war for the stability of Olivia's mental health, I got my wake-up call. I sat in front of an arts and crafts project at the treatment center where Olivia was living at the time. The project, titled "The Whole Person Wheel," was a simple pie chart cut into six slices, each slice labeled with one of six human potentials, what I considered basic human needs, like spirituality and physical health. Our task was to use crayons to color in the six slices of pie to the amount we thought we'd met our potential in each category. The project's purpose was simple — it was designed to show us what potentials required our attention, and to encourage us to make and meet goals to grow in the areas we needed to. The outcome, for me, was anything but simple.

When I finished coloring and put down my crayon, what I saw staring back at me was the depth of my shame and low self-esteem. My pie chart was filled with white, which signified unmet potentials. I had been so busy trying to fix my daughter that I had neglected to pay attention to what needed to be fixed within me. In that moment, I was forced to relinquish the fantasy that fixing her was within my control – nothing I had done thus far had helped Olivia and nothing I could in the future had any guarantee. I had to shift my focus off of her and onto me. Helping myself was the only option available to help her. My failure as a mother, if it could even be called a failure, had nothing to do with my daughter. Every decision I had made, I made with her best interest at heart. My failure as Olivia's mother was to not shower enough love upon myself, to not believe wholeheartedly about myself what I'd wanted my daughter to believe about herself: that I was enough. I needed to lead the way. I had no idea if redirecting my focus would solve anything, but I knew for sure I could not go on feeling as badly about myself as I felt.

So I did what I do best: I hit the books. I found books about shame. I learned what makes shame tick and implemented daily practices like gratitude and creativity to help me stop it in its tracks. I learned to identify shame's lies and how to dig for my truth. I learned the value of living a life of courage and started writing about our experiences. I found books about mindfulness, acceptance and letting go. I stopped hiding. I learned how to begin to control my emotions instead of letting them control me. I learned the value of paying acute attention to the present moment. I learned that my thoughts are not the sum of me. I reached out to friends I'd shied away from during our crisis. I practiced saying I was sorry, and meaning it. I connected with new friends and finally understood what it looked like to cultivate relationships. I forgave myself for the inherent flaws in my humanness. I found books about spirituality and adopted a non-traditional view of it. I became conscious to the amount of time I tried to numb myself with food. I did not lose weight, but I found a new way to appreciate my body. I looked for ways to be of service. I found empathy and compassion, for my daughter and for me. I worked on making these changes and believing in myself every day.

One month after I started learning how to be a better me, my daughter returned home at a normal weight, with appropriate eating habits, safe coping skills and with a new dedication to getting and staying mentally and physically healthy. She was not miraculously cured; there is no cure yet for mental illness. She came home determined to do the work required to obtain the life she wanted. Her resilience was a miracle and continues to be so today. Through my studies, I learned how to give her the space she needed to learn her own lessons in her own way. I learned how to be a woman of self-respect. I learned a new way to be present as a mother and to interact with integrity. Side by side we became happier and healthier than we'd ever been. This does not mean we didn't face setbacks. We did and still do. Setbacks are also the stuff of life — all of which is to say that I should not have been surprised to find myself standing in a tiny bathroom in a vacation condo in Hawaii with my old bathing suit stuck around my armpits and hateful thoughts towards my stomach lodged in my brain.

I stop staring at my stomach and take a couple of deep breaths to ground myself in my body, in this time and this place. I grab the suit top and yank it down. Begrudgingly it complies. I make a couple more unattractive maneuvers as I grab each boob and shove it into place and hook the strap around my neck. Phew. I wipe sweat off my forehead and remember the promise I made to myself. I understand this test as an opportunity to prove to myself that I'm not who I once was, and I allow the warmth of knowing to wash over me. The warmth comes from surviving the worst, and from forever changing for the better because of it. My gratitude erupts. My days of letting myself down are over. I step out of the bathroom and call out, "Who's ready to go to the beach?"

When Belly Shame is Medical, Too

MAYA SPIER STILES NORTH

Belly shame: women's hatred of their bellies; we hate the evidence of much of what makes us great — our ability to cradle life in our bodies and bring it forth into the world. What even the most "perfect" among us feel is hateful.

Is your tummy less than concave? Does it swell out gently? Does it carry the stretch marks of growth or childbirth? Does it vary from the perfect, airbrushed specimens portrayed in women's fashion magazines that even the models themselves cannot sport without actually trying to starve themselves to death?

Do you know that I would give almost anything to have the belly you despise? I don't just have a tummy. I am at peace with my stretch marks. But I don't just have a belly. I have what's called a "pannus" by some doctors. Wikipedia calls it a "panniculus".

You won't know I have it, generally. I've been dressing to hide it for 40 years. And you won't know by my Facebook profile picture, either — that's slender. Tiny even.

I had my beautiful daughter at 19. I was plump when I got pregnant, but less than half the size I would ultimately attain. My belly was loose and squishy, but honestly, it was more embarrassing than desolating. The skin was still young and tight, not terribly stretch-marked. Then I conceived, and, short as I am, with no room for the baby to grow but out, the skin stretched and stretched. Here's what most people don't know — stretch-marked skin is ruined skin. The elasticity is forever gone. It will never, ever snap back.

Over time, poverty, poor nutrition, fasting and dieting, and eating a lot when food was available (a typical response when one has gone hungry enough), I gained weight. The harder I tried — and I fasted on fruit juice, vitamins and protein powder so I wouldn't die from 30 to 47 days at a time — the more I gained, until I got myself up to a magnificent 420 pounds. On a 5'2" body.

At about 26, I was afraid to bend over. It felt like the skin on my legs and belly would split open if I did. Society is so brutal about being that size that I shut it off (think having trucks run at you as you're walking with grinning bastards yelling out the window "SooEEE!" or having herds of little boys follow you in stores, pointing, laughing and shouting "Fatty, fatty, fatty!"). I shut it down. I didn't even see it because to see it would have brought me down, and I had a child to raise.

Until I couldn't not see it.

It was shoved into my face in such a way as I could not look away. Absolutely horrified, I proceeded to lose 225 pounds. And when I was done, the belly was still there, covering my mons, resting on my upper thighs, cutting off circulation.

Statistics on people keeping the weight off for five years or more are brutal — 95 percent of people fail, as did I, although not entirely. I kept it off for a few months, then over time, went up to 365 again, then down, then up. I took up power-lifting and got down to 340, with an astonishing muscle mass so I looked quite a bit smaller. Then down to 295, then up. Then martial arts and down at one point to 275. And always, always, the panniculus was there. Hurting me. Resting on a place that has now long since gone painfully numb (surprisingly, not an oxymoron) with ridges of fatty tumors from 40 years of pressure. Sometimes, at my job as a computer programmer, I discreetly put my fists under it just so the blood could rush back into my legs and because it ached so terribly where all that pressure rested.

Finally, with my doctor's encouragement, I admitted to myself that literally nothing I had done to lose this weight was really ever going to work — I couldn't seem to get below 275 at all and even then, not for more than a few days (literally!).

Two years ago, May 28, 2013, I underwent gastric bypass surgery and the weight began to melt off. The best I have attained was 196, but after weighing 420, that's a happy number. I've had some rebound weight (they warn us about it), so I'm currently at 209. I wear between a size 14 and 16, which after a 30/32 is also a pretty happy number.

But not only is my panniculus still there, it hangs lower, still presses on my legs. It hurts. I get fungal and staph infections where the skin gets no air. My navel sags so much now that it, too, gets painful infections. I routinely fold up a small square of tissue to keep it dry – what it absorbs is a darkish brown. I'm afraid to find out what it is. Sometimes my back really hurts from the extra weight —

this is no small thing, no little, wrinkly pooch which you at least wouldn't notice when I'm clothed. This thing is a monster.

I had assumed that the infections would mean its removal would be covered. After all, I'd done what was required. The weight is gone, as much as it's going to go. I've worked so very hard for this. I had the infections documented. According to another friend who also had the gastric bypass, her doctors said that more than a Coke can of extra skin was a medical issue. Can we say bucket? But no, according to my insurance, this is merely cosmetic.

Sure it is, if you mean that I'm so ashamed at the hideousness of my body that, should my husband predecease me, I will never have the courage to find another love ever again. Sure it is if you mean that I look down at this ghastly, hanging deformity and have vivid imaginings of taking a kitchen knife and sawing it off, even if I bled to death because at least, for a few moments, it would at last be gone (no, I won't, but I've talked to other women who have this and so far we've all had this vision).

But it's more. As I said, it gets infections. It cuts off the circulation in my legs, contributing to intense swelling in my lower limbs (I know, because when I lie down and the panniculus slithers back and to my sides, I can feel the fluid rushing back upward). It's created that numb spot. God only knows what's growing in my belly button.

The common treatment is an abdominoplasty — a "tummy tuck." I don't even need that. A tummy tuck involves shortening the abdominal muscles that are commonly stretched out. I am a perfect muscular specimen in a squid suit. My abdominal muscles are tight, flat and hard as steel as are all my muscles thanks to years of power lifting and martial arts and other athletic pursuits. And while I despise the ruin left when my triple chin emptied out (it's asymmetrical — it drives me nuts!), and I'm none too delighted with my arms as aeronautical devices, those truly are cosmetic.

Despite an appeal to my insurance company, which was denied, this pannus, or panniculus, is not cosmetic. It really isn't. It's been between a Grade 2, as it is now, to very nearly a Grade 4 (as determined by a Wikipedia article). The cost to fix it with only the panniculectomy I need? Nine thousand dollars. I don't have it and my insurance won't cover it.

My ultimate questions are: If it didn't have to do with fat, would insurance companies be so quick to dismiss it as cosmetic? And does this perhaps put your sweet, rounded tummy into perspective a bit?

Free at last from my apron of fat

When I first wrote about belly shame for iPinion Syndicate's website, In fear and trembling, I took pictures of the enormous panniculus — the apron of fat — that had caused me so much physical pain and discomfort, not to mention a belly shame so epic that the self-loathing climbed my soul like a giant ape that has taken residence in the upper stories of a tall building. I was told that I was brave to show it. In a culture that demands physical perfection well into old age, I suppose exposing something so deeply imperfect could be seen that way, but it seemed long overdue to speak my truth about it. It wasn't as if I could truly hide it. And it wasn't as if I was the only one, either.

There are a number of surgeries used to divest a body of a panniculus. What I needed was a panniculectomy. Some people get abdominoplasties, which also involve cutting and shortening the abdominal muscles. I didn't need that. Years of athletics have given me tight, steely muscles underneath my squid suit.

I had taken several runs at convincing my HMO that this was not cosmetic — although there is, of course, a cosmetic element to it. The damned thing rested on my legs, cutting off circulation, creating numb, painful patches on my thighs. It got dreadful fungal and occasional bacterial infections, but after a lifetime, I was able to keep those down to a minimum. The HMO's requirement for consideration hinged mainly on having an intransigent bacterial infection that required internal antibiotics and two office visits. I also had to be a certain time past my gastric bypass with stabilized weight, but it was the requirement for an infection that stymied me most.

Seriously? I had spent 40 years preventing infections! I wore underpants several sizes too large and tucked them everywhere flesh met flesh, every place that could generate an infection. I'd had enough of them to know they had to be prevented. They were horrible — miserable, tunneling infections that raised my blood sugar along with my temperature and made me really sick. And I was supposed to allow that in order to prove I needed surgery to prevent it?

I wrote my primary care physician, a doctor so good she apparently has a waiting list, that it was flat-out foolhardiness to expect a diabetic to allow an infection that would damage her health in order to prove a need for surgery to prevent just that. Bless her common sense and my columnist's writing skills. She replied, "You're right. It's absolute foolishness. I'll back you up!"

Thus encouraged, despite the initial denial of my first request and subsequent appeal, back I went to the plastic surgeon, who told me rather glumly that it was an absolute waste of time and of his staff's resources to try again.

"We have to try again," I told him. "Third time's a charm. If it doesn't go through this time, I'll explore other options, but we simply must. And if we get turned down, I'm writing the Insurance Commissioner with all my mad columnist skills to make a great deal of noise because this is bigotry. I'm pretty sure if this wasn't fat related, they would be far less reluctant to cover it." After all, you want plastic surgery? Have a mastectomy! You can get brand new boobies for free because, after all, what is a woman without boobies? Seriously — as far as I know, you can get reconstructed before you even wake up from the mastectomy!

The lovely plastic surgeon sighed and acquiesced. He would start the process again. He would send his recommendation that this was truly necessary, complete with pictures, but he held out little hope.

That was May 29. Late June, the letter came. The surgery was authorized. I must have read it three times, terrified that all it said was that I was retroactively authorized for the initial exam, but no, it was for the surgery. It really was. I literally doubled over and sobbed. Forty years. Imagine it. Forty years.

I called the surgeon's office the very next day and took the first possible date: July 8. Miraculously, I had the leave from work.

I confess, I had a few moments where I seriously questioned why the hell I would put myself through surgery and recovery again. Surgery HURTS. But 40 years of pain — even all the pain of recovery doesn't compare if you consider 40 years of pure misery.

I made my arrangements. My daughter offered her one-story home and TLC for the initial stages of my recovery. I brought two Chihuahuas for comfort.

I wore overalls to the hospital and my daughter put my hair into two tiny braids. I was cheerful throughout the whole process, and giggled through the surgeon marking my belly up with a purple marker (it tickled!). They wheeled my bed into the operating room. I smiled at the people looming over me and —

My eyes opened.

I was numb and dizzy and disoriented. The nurse was kind. Did my family come in? Yeah, they must have — my daughter took a picture to prove I had survived and posted it on Facebook. I got well wishes and wrote garble. My daughter tells me I discussed elephants and lifted my boobies and announced I still had cleavage.

The next day, I went to my daughter's house. And oh, it hurt.

The hernia operation — no biggie. The gastric bypass, not even painful within a week. This? Oh My Freaking God. It's been 15 days and it still hurts. The incision is *epic*. It goes from behind one hip to behind the other. I look like I nearly got cut in half then got reattached again. My tummy is swollen. My daughter informed me, with an embarrassed snicker, that I looked like a frog.

I also have no belly button.

But — It's *gone*. This damned fecking panniculus, this thing that hurt and screwed with my back and was hideous and mortifying — it's GONE! I look down at legs. I can see my female bits for the first time in 40 years. (I have BITS???)

And now, at least in clothes, I actually look normal. I'm not thin, but I'm really not what most people would consider fat. I get smiles, and greeted as if I was just anybody because now I am. I don't weigh over 400 pounds. I don't have a huge belly that jiggles and bulges and flaps when I run. I just look like anybody.

It still pisses me off that I had to literally transform myself to be considered human again, but at the same time, I'd be lying if I was to say I wasn't beyond delighted by this brand new life. I'm crafting my crone, my elder, my old bat and believe me, my honeys, she's gonna fly.

And where my belly button is supposed to be, I'm getting a mandala tattoo.

Life without the belly — adventures
in keeping my pants up

The time slide is an interesting thing. It's a spiral slide, in my experience, and it's several stories tall. You start out at a decent pace — and then you hit the slick spots and ye gods, off you go. One minute I was struggling to even get the surgery. The next minute, I'm here, sans belly flap.

I had my panniculectomy — the removal of my panniculus or apron of belly fat — about six weeks ago. I've concluded that I'm no longer intrigued by the bizarre leap between the moment they put you under and the moment you come out of anesthesia. Nonetheless, of all my remodels, and despite the incredible and wonderful transformation afforded me by the gastric bypass, this panniculectomy was without a doubt the most desperately yearned-for surgery of my life.

Now, 48 days since surgery, to be precise, the pain is gone. What's numb is numb and the amputated nerves are no longer outraged. Oh, it all burned there for a while. Naturally, being the tank that I am, I was back at work at the end of the second week of surgery and it was a challenge to do much. Essentially, I'd been skinned, a chunk amputated and the edges stitched back together. The scar is epic. I guarantee you that no little kid is ever going to beat me in a "wanna see my scars?" contest.

What's it like now, living without the evil belly which, I'm willing to bet, probably weighed upwards of 80 or 90 pounds when I was at my heaviest, 420 pounds? Walking is easier. I didn't exactly expect that, but even the 11 pounds they took off wiggled and wobbled and weighed on my legs. Climbing stairs required lifting that extra weight with each step. Well, that makes sense, but it still came as a surprise. When I walk, I feel my anatomy, uncloaked, in motion. It was always occluded. Now it's not.

I was always oddly flexible. At well over 300 pounds, I could bend over and put my hands flat on the ground (freaked the snot out of the less flexible among my slender friends). Now? It's crazy. I can bend over flat against my knees. When lounging in my chair-and-a-half, I can fold my leg back and play with my toes (if I was so inclined, although my toes hold no fascination for me) or I can curl up with my knees under my chin, a la 5 year old. Once in position, my tribe of pets arrange themselves all around me and there's plenty of room.

People were still looking away from me before the panniculectomy — nowhere near the way they did when I weighed over 300 pounds, but there was no hiding the panniculus and deformities (that's essentially what it was) both intrigue and repel people. Now, I'm normal. Okay, at least when clothed. Out of clothes, I still have jelly thighs (epic loose skin, but all cosmetic) and due to being almost unnaturally short-coupled (think an inch and a half between top of hip bone and bottom rib), I do resemble a bullfrog. My arms are rather disappointing aeronautical devices (no amount of flapping gets me off the ground — what a bummer!). But in clothes, I just look normal.

That's a new one on me

Am I delighted? Oh geez — not even a book contains enough words to express how much. However, there's one unexpected side effect that I had no idea would be so annoying.

My pants fall down.

As it turns out, the panniculus was what was keeping my pants up all these years. I had no idea! I found this out early in my recovery when my granddaughter and I went to the small town of Tenino, Washington, to go to a rock show with Granddad.

Now, I love cargo pants. I'm an odd blend of feminine and "not so much," so I love cargos and I particularly love men's cargos because the pockets are just way, way better. I'm now wearing size 36 to 38 men's cargos, with the 38s being kind of big and 36s being a bit tight (figures). So I put on the 38s and down they started to slide. Well, that wouldn't do, so I put on the 36s (this before I discovered the magic of belts). They were just this side of miserably tight and they had an inner tie, so I thought they would do.

Not so much.

Tight or no, those pants started their descent as soon as I got out of the car, not to mention they slid down and pressed — hard — on that very very very newly healed scar. Naturally it never occurred to me to pack an alternative outfit. Oh no, that would've been thinking ahead.

So, I was walking around, looking at exquisite stones of all sorts and every few feet I was desperately and painfully hitching up the pants — ow, ow, ow. Walk a few feet — hitch. Walk a few more feet — HITCH. Somehow, they survived the circuit, but it became apparent that I was losing the battle. We were spent anyway. I gave Sophia (my glorious granddaughter) a desperate look and said, "We need to go home, honey, I'm in trouble here."

We took off at a rapid toddle toward the car, me clutching one side of my pants as I dealt with the secondary consequence of all this — my backpack was riding my shirt higher and higher in back, which consequently pulled it up in front. I was being involuntarily denuded by the clothes themselves, right in the middle of beautiful downtown Tenino!

We reached the car just in the nick of time. I dropped the backpack, huddled close to the car, unzipped and pulled up the pants (which also HURT) and made the dash for home and a kinder, gentler outfit.

Later, safely installed under the giant, spreading Mother Walnut tree, Sophia observed that those were "the Pants of Embarrassment."

"Indeed," I concurred, "to go with the Shirt of Mortification," and she laughed.

God, I love having a granddaughter who, at 12, knows what the word "mortification" means.

Our contributors

Carolyn Wyler

I am an empty nester mother of four boys, stepmom to three girls and two boys, grandmother to eight and a full time Registered nurse. Although I am somewhat shy in nature, I often turn to my left side of my brain to express what I can't always verbalize and to escape from the stresses of reality. From painting, decorating cakes or writing, I like to create images or ideas that are a bit outside of the box. I am attracted to the weird, the crazy, colorful and unusual (which is probably why her number one love and most important thing in her life is her family).

Christy Sillman

Having been born with complex congenital heart defects, I wasn't sure what I'd be able to accomplish in my predicted short life. Today, in my mid-30s and with an adjusted life expectancy into my 80s, I'm a mother, a wife, an accomplished masters prepared nurse, and an advocate for patients living congenital heart disease. I enjoy hiking, crochet, binge-watching TV, drawing, painting and coloring. Ultimately, I'm a storyteller, and I hope you enjoy my personal thoughts, quirky tales and unique perspective on life.

David Lacy

I began writing for The Davis Enterprise in 1995. My weekly column, "Growing Younger," began in 1999, and won first place in the California Newspaper Publishers Association's Better Newspapers Contest in 2003. I have a BA in English from UC Davis with highest honors and an M.A. in English from UC Irvine. I teach college in Southern California. I am iPinion's co-founder and serve as C.O.O. I am also a contributor to Elite Daily. Originally from Northern California, I currently reside in Orange County with my wife and two dogs.

Debra DeAngelo

I have been writing a weekly column for McNaughton Newspapers for 23 years, and have won multiple state and national awards for my columns. I've served as a California Newspaper Publishers Association judge in the annual Better Newspapers Contest for 21 years and am the co-founder, co-editor and CEO for iPinion Syndicate, an online group of award winning writers, columnist, bloggers and photographers. I have two grown children who survived my (s)mothering and live in Winters, California with The Cutest Man In The World (a.k.a. my husband) and two crazy cats. I am the managing editor of the local newspaper, the Winters Express. I also write about Napa Valley wine tasting adventures via Highway 128 (Eastern Gateway to the Napa Valley — trademark mine).

Donald Sanders

My people come from Tennessee, some Southerners, and some Yankees. I'm a student of ancestry and have traced my ancestors as far back as Jamestown in 1610. Unfortunately I found out he was a cannibal. I come from a long line of disabled veterans so I had to follow suit. I live in Winters, California, where I write a column for the local newspaper, the Winters Express. I am married to Therese; we have three children and two grandchildren. I have a very large brain.

Hannah Sullivan

I am just your somewhat average 20-something, dog-loving ChapStick addict living in Rhode Island. After years of deliberation and hard work, I am finally in the home stretch of getting my English degree. When I'm not procrastinating or attending $2 taco night, you can find me writing columns and watching "Doctor Who." Hoarding graphic novels, finding the perfect pineapple salsa and winged eyeliner are my passions in life. All of my inspiration comes directly from any and all dysfunctions in my life so, it is safe to assume I will never run out of things to write about.

Judith Newton

I'm a Professor Emerita at UC Davis, where I directed the Women and Gender Studies Program and the Consortium for Women and Research. My memoir, "Tasting Home: Coming of Age in the Kitchen," was published in March of 2013 by She Writes Press and has won twelve independent press awards. I'm working on a feminist mystery entitled "Oink!" and, in my academic days, I published five works of nonfiction on nineteenth century women writers, feminist criticism, women in history, and mens' movements. I live in the Bay Area and cook for non-profit benefits and for family and friends.

Kathie Yount

In 2010, I was living an ordinary life as a retired English teacher and antiques shop co-owner. All that changed on February 16 when my son took his life in San Francisco. I had been expecting grandchildren, but I got "suicide baiting" instead, which is how my son died — publicly and irrationally in front of 1,000 people, including those who were openly provoking his death by taunting him and yelling "JUMP!" I write to raise awareness about the psychological anomaly of suicide baiting and to lobby for better police training in their interactions with the despondent at the suicide attempt scene.

Kathleen Brotherton

I reside in the lovely town of Greenwich, Connecticut, nestled along the eastern seaboard. I am the mom to three children, Brittany, Joseph and Jordan, who are respectively eight years spaced makes for a life rich in adventure. This year, the addition of Kali Bey brought the blessing of becoming an "Amma." Young adult issues are my great passion, and this passion led me to spearhead the "Young Columnists" section of iPinion, which gives young people a forum to speak their voice. I am also passionate about fiction writing. In 2015, two of my short stories were published in anthologies. As a writer, I wear many hats: columnist, author, blogger and photographer. Bring on the next project, as I'm always looking for something to help create!

Kelvin Wade

I'm a 40-something Northern California freelance writer who has been writing an opinion column for the Fairfield Daily Republic for more than 20 years. My first Daily Republic column, written while in junior high, ran from 1979-80. I've also produced newsletters, flyers and other publications for numerous associations from Roseville to Pacific Grove, California. My first two short story ebooks, "Morsels: Twisted Tales of Life and Death" (Vol. 1 and 2), are available online. I was a founder of the Bay Area Survivors of Suicide following my brother's suicide. I'm devoted to my significantly better half, Cathi, and our two lovely pooches.

Maya Spier Stiles North

All my life, I have been seduced by words — their beauty, their power, their ability to transform lives and cultures. Words gave me sanctuary in the worst of times — when I was a street kid, in a juvenile institution, when I got married at 17, had my daughter at 19. They helped me transform experience into what approaches wisdom (as best I can) as I became a writer, a copy editor, an artist and computer programmer. In fact, my words had the power to tick off Bill O'Reilly to the point where he invited me to interview with him on national TV and personally promise me he would get his rabies shot beforehand. For me, being an iPinioneer is the fruition of a life dream and is allowing me to use my words as a force for good, for change, for evolution.

Tom McMasters-Stone

It's one of the great honors of my life to have been asked to join this august group of people at iPinion. Ostensibly, I cover politics, but I may write about anything. I have written extensively about my struggles with alcohol, which I now know was powered by severe childhood PTSD and a weak enzyme in my brain. Both are being treated successfully, and while constituting a disability, they are no longer disabling. I am happily married to my second wife, Carol, and have four great children. I am a retired firefighter, and I have Associate and Bachelor's degrees. I am very grateful for the people who take the time to read my columns.

Tracey Yokas

I'm a mom, wife, friend and writer with a passion for connection. I aspire to write my deepest truth so that others will know they are not alone and to eradicate the stigma and ignorance that surround mental illness. I volunteer as a teacher for my local NAMI's Family To Family class and, in an effort to keep NAMI's programs free to the public, I've bugged enough friends and family to be a top ten individual fundraiser for two years. I hold a BS in Communications from Ohio University and a MS in Counseling Psychology from California Lutheran University. I'm working on my first memoir and live in Southern California with my husband, daughter and two totally awesome cats.

www.ingramcontent.com/pod-product-compliance
Lightning Source LLC
Chambersburg PA
CBHW062020280526
45787CB00005B/2178